Journey
to Jerusalem

2002-3 NMI
MISSION EDUCATION RESOURCES

✻ ✻ ✻

READING BOOKS

ADVENTURE WITH GOD
The Jeanine van Beek Story
by Helen Temple

HANDS FOR THE HARVEST
Laborers for the Lord in the Far East
by A. Brent Cobb

JOURNEY TO JERUSALEM
Making a Difference in the Middle East
by Pat Stockett Johnston

MOZAMBIQUE MOMENTS
E-mail from the African Bush
by Douglas J. Perkins and Phyllis H. Perkins

TRIUMPH IN TRINIDAD
God's Promises Never Failed
by Ruth O. Saxon

UNDER THE "L"
Mission Field Chicago
by L. Wayne Hindmand

✻ ✻ ✻

ADULT MISSION EDUCATION RESOURCE BOOK

CALLED TO TEACH
Edited by Wes Eby

Journey
to Jerusalem
Making a Difference
in the Middle East

by

Pat Stockett Johnston

NPH

Nazarene Publishing House
Kansas City, Missouri

Copyright 2002
by Nazarene Publishing House

ISBN 083-411-9692

Printed in the United States of America

Editor: Wes Eby
Cover Design: Michael Walsh

10   9   8   7   6   5   4   3   2   1

Dedication

Schools have greatly enabled the Church of the Nazarene to make a difference in the Middle East. Therefore, I gratefully dedicate this book to those who had the vision to open and direct Nazarene schools in this area of the world.

- Rev. Mulhim Thahabiyah*—Arabic school, Bludan, Syria, 1922
- Rev. Samuel Krikorian—Armenian school, Jerusalem, Palestine, 1924; Ashrafiyya Armenian school, Amman, Jordan, 1948; Ashrafiyya Arabic school, Beirut, Lebanon, 1950
- Rev. Don DePasquale—Arabic school, Damascus, Syria, 1946; Sin-el-Fil Armenian school, Beirut, Lebanon, 1956
- Rev. Nerses Sarian—Armenian school, Damascus, Syria, 1946
- Mrs. Yevigne Chamichian—Ashrafiyya Armenian school, Amman, Jordan, 1948
- Rev. William Russell—Arabic school, Zerka, Jordan, 1948
- Dr. Donald Reed—Beirut Bible College, Beirut, Lebanon, 1954

---

*A guide on pages 86-88 provides pronunciation of unfamiliar words.

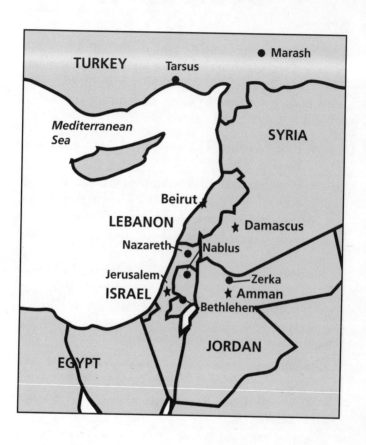

Contents

Pat Stockett Johnston and her husband, Gordon, are career missionaries for the Church of the Nazarene. Since 1969, they have served in Lebanon, Papua New Guinea, and Jordan (two different times). The Johnstons return to the United States in July of 2002 for a year of deputation and retirement at Casa Robles.

Pat is the director of Arabic publications for the Eastern Mediterranean Field. As a freelance writer, she has had articles published in *Holiness Today, World Mission, Herald of Holiness,* and *Come Ye Apart.* She is author of *Is That You, God?* a 2001-2 adult NMI reading book; *Changed Hearts, Changed Lives,* a 1994-95 adult NMI reading book; and *City of Fear,* a 1999—2000 children's mission book.

Pat received her B.A. from Pasadena/Point Loma Nazarene University and her M.A. from California State University, Los Angeles. She is an ordained minister in the Church of the Nazarene.

Foreword

As most people know, the Middle East is perhaps the most fascinating place on earth. Others may disagree, but I find the historic, cultural, political, and religious streams that flow through that part of our globe to be filled with intrigue, delight, and discovery.

Even the name itself can be intriguing and confusing and contradictory. In some places the Middle East is called the Near East. In other places the Middle East is called West Asia. It has been identified as Oriental, and yet, not really. Nor is it really Middle East. It is what it is. It is what we think it to be. That is the nature of the area. Confusing, often frustrating, but always fascinating, with fascinating people who have fascinating stories.

Anyone who knows Pat Stockett Johnston will long remember her. Throughout her career she has entered into every assignment with passion, energy, enthusiasm, and singular devotion. Her abiding legacy will be literature, both the production of it and the writing of it. She has built systems of literature production in at least two distinct areas of the world, including the most recent in Arabic. These will outlive any of us who read these pages.

Pat has entered into some of the lives of those who have most impacted the work of our church in this part of the world through education. Hardly any greater tool or technique can be found to mold, shape, and create the future than educating our young (and old too, for that matter). So, Pat has wedded a great area of the world with great people, who have helped place the contours on the church as it exists today.

Read. Enjoy. Benefit. Rejoice.

—R. Franklin Cook
Eurasia regional director

Acknowledgments

I did not write this book alone. In fact, if I had not had the fantastic support and cooperation of the lead characters in each chapter, the book would not exist.

Berge Najarian was the Holy Land district superintendent when Gordon and I arrived in Beirut in 1969. Doris and he made brief visits to Beirut during those first years. But I never discussed his early history. Only when I discovered he had been a student at the Jerusalem Armenian Evangelical Protestant School did I E-mail him for more details. The story of his family's journey to Jerusalem inspired me to submit a prospectus for a book built around Nazarene schools in the Middle East. Thank you, Berge.

Accounts of William and Grace Russell's missionary career in Palestine and Jordan are told in two past NMI reading books: The first, *Jerusalem and Beyond* by Alice Spangenberg in 1950; the second, *The Nations and the Isles* by Olive G. Tracy in 1958. Our assignments to Jordan from 1976 to 1980 and then from 1995 to 2002 enabled me to see the fruits of the Russells' labor. A 1999 visit with William Russell in Brixham, Devon, England, inspired me to include not just William and Grace's story but also share about some of the fruit their sacrifice produced in the Middle East. Thank you, William.

Except for growth in population, dusty Zerka hasn't changed one whit since Jirair Tashjian, along with his four brothers and parents, Samuel and Helen, lived in the ground-floor apartment on the Nazarene property. I happened upon an article by Jirair in the May—June 1998 issue of *Flame* magazine in which he testified to the positive influence of the Nazarene church and school on his life. He particularly mentioned the ministry of the Russells. Again, E-mail opened the door to more details from Jirair and his brother Kegham. Thank you both.

When we left war-torn Beirut in 1975, we didn't know when we would return. In 1996 we had the opportunity to again visit the city we love and meet with Nazarene Sin-el-Fil school principal, Abdo Khanashot, and his assistant, Marlene Mchantaf. Thank you, Abdo, for your faithfulness during 15 years of civil war. And thank you, Marlene, for so willingly sharing your testimony.

The Zerka Nazarene church celebrated its 50th anniversary in 2000. During the ceremony, Dr. Alex Abu Ghazaleh told of the influence of the school and church on his life. He later agreed to be interviewed, and I spent a morning in his clinic recording his memories of Zerka and the Russells. Thank you, Alex, for letting me tell your story.

During the interview, Alex mentioned his contact with a couple who had recently emigrated to Canada. I thank Munir and Amera for allowing their story to be included.

A final thanks goes to Dr. Lynn Neil from Northwest Nazarene University, who gave up hours of her Cyprus vacation when editing my chapters with her famous red and green squiggles.

Introduction

Call it civil unrest. Call it religious persecution. Call it war. Think about people on the run. People fleeing bombs and bullets. People searching for safety. Label them as displaced persons. As refugees. As jobless. Frightened. Lost. Remember that many of them never got to go back home again.

And what did such conflict, such turmoil, produce? The ingredients . . . the climate . . . the opportunity for the opening and continued growth of the Church of the Nazarene in the Middle East.

In *Journey to Jerusalem* you will read about

- Samuel and Guelenia Najarian and their hurried escape from Marash, Turkey, in 1919, and arrival in Jerusalem;

- Rebecca Krikorian, who had to discard a plan for a Christian mission in her home of Aintab, Turkey, after a new wave of persecution against Christians hit in 1895;

- Samuel Krikorian and his aunt Rebecca's desire to serve in Jerusalem;

- William and Grace Russell and war's effect on their ministries in the Middle East;

- Samuel and Helen Tashjian, who escaped the Armenian massacres in Tarsus, Turkey, and finally settled in Zerka, Jordan;

- Marlene Mchantaf's story, colored by the 1975-90 Lebanese Civil War;

- Alex Abu Ghazaleh and his family's flight from Ramleh, Palestine, during the Arab-Israeli War of 1948, and how they became neighbors to the Nazarenes in Zerka, Jordan;
- Munir and Amera who fled, not from enemy fire, but from a ruthless dictator and his reign of terror.

Through all of these historical events God worked to bring these people in relationship to himself. The Nazarenes whose stories are related here represent the Church of the Nazarene in the Middle East in the past and today. God has used and continues to use them to make a difference in their world.

1
Journey to Jerusalem

Guelenia never planned to journey to Jerusalem during her growing-up years. After all, her father, Megerditch Amiralian, was a wealthy Armenian merchant in Marash, Turkey. Guelenia was raised in a Protestant home and converted as a teenager in the Armenian Gregorian Church. And although she realized some tension existed between the minority Christian Armenian population and the Muslim Turks, the conflict had never been enough to force her to leave her hometown. Not yet.

■ ■ ■

**Guelenia's father chose death
over denying Christ.**

■ ■ ■

Life for Armenians living under Islam had never been easy. After Islamic armies conquered the Middle East in the seventh century, the persecution of Armenians began and later intensified under the Egyptian Mamluks and Ottoman Turks. The latter group was determined to absorb the Armenian population into the Turkish culture and Islamic religion. In the 1800s German and later American Congregational missionaries came to evangelize the Turks, but with little success; therefore, they started working among the Armenians living in Turkey. In 1895 the Turkish government, wanting to demoralize the Armenian population once again, began a new wave of torturing and killing Christian leaders who would not convert to Islam. At age 55, Guelenia's father chose death over denying Christ. Somehow, her mother was able to hold the family together.

Guelenia married Samuel Najarian, who was not a born-again believer, in 1900. The year before Samuel married, he had graduated from the American missionary-run Syrian Protestant College (later the American University of Beirut), located in what is now Lebanon, with a master of pharmacy degree. He then returned to Marash to work. Two sons and a daughter were born in the first six years of marriage.

In 1918 at the end of World War I, part of Turkey was awarded to French Syria; thus, French troops occupied the area, including Guelenia's hometown of Marash. Turkish bandits and outlaws created havoc, however, and as the winter of 1919 approached, the French withdrew. The Armenians in Marash realized their only hope of survival was to abandon their homes and possessions and flee.

The Najarians—Guelenia; her husband, Samuel; their children, Albert, Angel, and Higazoon; and Samuel's father, Ohan—joined other refugees in fleeing the country, knowing they faced immediate death if caught by the Turks. During the Najarians' flight they became separated from 13-year-old Higazoon and Samuel's 85-year-old father. The old man and his grandson did not survive the march; no one knows if their deaths were caused by the rigors of the journey or if they were murdered.

A fierce snowstorm wrapped the miserable Armenian refugees in its deadly white embrace during their exodus to Turkey's seacoast. Samuel and Guelenia trudged in the freezing cold with Albert and Angel for four days with only short rests, meager food, and snow for water. (It is estimated that 20,000 Armenians followed the French out of Marash. Only 4,000 survived, since many who escaped annihilation by the Turks froze to death along the way.) The Najarians didn't realize it, but they had begun their journey to Jerusalem.

The Najarians made their way to Beirut, Lebanon, where Samuel was able to contact a former college classmate who worked as a pharmacist in Khartoum, Sudan. Samuel accepted a job offer to work with his friend, and the family moved to northeastern Africa. While here their second daughter, Louise, was born and their surviving son, Albert, emigrated to the United States.

Later when it became obvious there was insufficient work in the Khartoum pharmacy for two pharmacists, Samuel and Guelenia moved to Cairo, Egypt, with their daughters. Another son, Berge, was born in Cairo on Christmas Eve 1924. Angel married and also moved to America. Life was hard in Egypt because Samuel, a refugee with an American mission-sponsored college degree, could not obtain a license to practice pharmacy.

Ever since her marriage in 1900, Guelenia had prayed for Samuel's conversion. While in Egypt she heard that an American Evangelical Holiness mission in Jerusalem had started a work among Armenian refugees from Turkey. "O God," she prayed, "would you open doors for us to move to Jerusalem?" She wanted her family to attend this holiness church, although she didn't even know its name.

With the help of a relative of the Najarians in Joppa, God answered her petition by getting Samuel a job offer as a pharmacist in Jerusalem, and he went by himself to check it out. Palestine was under British Mandate at that time, and the government recognized Samuel's Beirut training and licensed him to practice pharmacy.

This "holiness mission" Guelenia had heard about was the Armenian Church of the Nazarene.

✳   ✳   ✳

God had used another Armenian from Turkey, Samuel Krikorian, to do the impossible—open a Protestant Armenian work in the city of Jerusalem.

■ ■ ■

Samuel, unknowingly, had taken the first steps on his journey to Jerusalem.

■ ■ ■

Samuel was born in Aintab, Turkey, in 1893. When he was two years old, his aunt, Rebecca Krikorian, went to the United States to raise funds for a Christian mission in Turkey. The new wave of massacres of Armenians took place shortly after she left,

Rev. Samuel Krikorian, 1921

and opportunities for Christian missions in Turkey closed. For years she sought to arrange for Samuel to come to the States to live with her, finally succeeding in 1909. Samuel, unknowingly, had taken the first steps on his journey to Jerusalem. Aunt Rebecca came in contact with the Church of the Nazarene during her travels around the United States. When she suggested that Samuel attend the Nazarene college in Pasadena, California, he enrolled, graduated in 1917, and joined the Church of the Nazarene.

Both Samuel and his aunt Rebecca felt God's call to open a mission in Jerusalem, so they approached the Nazarene Foreign Missions Board about starting a work there. The Church of the Nazarene approved the project in 1919 and appointed both aunt and nephew to go to Jerusalem. When health problems made it impossible for Rebecca to make the journey, Samuel held deputation services for two years and then sailed for Palestine in August of 1921. Whether the Church of the Nazarene would be granted permission to start a Protestant work in Jerusalem was touch and go for a while, since the British occupation authorities insisted the church agree to operate an orphanage before being granted a permit to open a new mission. Fred Parker in *Mission to the World* tells what happened next:

> Shortly after receiving this news [about an orphanage], Dr. H. F. Reynolds, general superintendent and general secretary of Foreign Missions, visited Jerusalem. When apprised of the problem, Dr. Reynolds suggested they spend a night of prayer concerning the matter out on the Mount of Olives, which they did. With the dawn came the assurance in their hearts that God was moving on their behalf. Indeed, within a few days the orphanage project was taken over by another group, and the church was granted the necessary permit to launch a mission. Rev. Krikorian set to work immediately, and during the ensuing year moved among the refugees, gathering a nucleus for a church.[1]

Rev. Alvin and Naomi Kauffman transferred to Jerusalem from India in 1922 to help establish the church. Parker continues:

> With the help of the rector of the Anglican

church, a building was rented near the Jaffa Gate on the road to Bethlehem, and regular services were begun in December 1922. On April 6, 1924, the Church of the Nazarene was officially organized with 21 members.[2]

A month before the organization of the church, Samuel Krikorian married Hranoush Yardumian, a Beirut schoolteacher. At first many of the Nazarene children attended a Roman Catholic school. However, a recent ruling had been made by the priest that all Catholic school students were required to attend Sunday services in the Catholic church. The solution? The Nazarenes had to open a school of their own. Hranoush and her sister, Puzantohie, helped start an elementary school in connection with the new Nazarene church.

Immediately upon returning to Jerusalem from

First Nazarene congregation in Jerusalem.
Rev. Krikorian is on far left. Circa 1922.

Samuel and Hranoush Krikorian (seated in middle) with teachers
and students at Nazarene school in Jerusalem, 1935.

furlough in 1928, Alvin Kauffman negotiated the
price of only $12,000 for a choice 100' x 200' lot in
the New City on Julian Way, directly across from a
million-dollar YMCA building and near King David
Hotel. A multipurpose, two-story, stone building was
constructed at the back of the lot. The lower floor
contained classrooms; the second floor was the
Krikorians' residence. The area between the building
and the main road was a playground where a large
sanctuary would be built after the funds were raised.

* * *

In the fall of 1929 after Samuel Najarian found
work in Jerusalem, Guelenia and her two youngest
children, Louise and Berge, traveled by train from
Cairo to join him. The family rented an apartment
several blocks from the Old City in west Jerusalem.

Their home was in walking distance of the Armenian Church of the Nazarene they had come so far to attend. They were delighted to discover that the Nazarenes ran a kindergarten and elementary school called the Armenian Evangelical Protestant School and quickly enrolled Louise and Berge.

Rev. Krikorian was both the pastor of the Nazarene church and acting principal of the school. Surprisingly, the Najarians had always spoken English with their children; therefore, Louise and Berge learned English in an Armenian home and Armenian in an American school. Several years later Guelenia's husband, Samuel Najarian, accepted the Lord in this Jerusalem Nazarene Church. He became a strong believer and served as secretary of the church board for many years.

Berge Najarian clearly remembers his days as a student at the Armenian Evangelical Protestant School. "Kindergarten was taught in Armenian, and in grades one through six, Armenian was used for Bible and memory work as well as Armenian history and language," he says. "English and Arabic were also taught as languages. Before morning devotions, we students would line up in our light blue uniforms—knee-length dresses for the girls and short pants with uniform shirts for the boys—and hold out our hands. A handkerchief held by our thumbs and index fingers was stretched open with hands apart. One of the teachers would come and check our fingernails, faces, ears, hair, and handkerchiefs for cleanness. We knew what discipline was!

"We had 20-minute recesses in the morning and

afternoon and the lunch break was 90 minutes. If we lived close enough we were allowed to go home at noon. However, many students brought sandwiches, hard-boiled eggs, and fruit to school. Christmas programs were a big production, with most of the students taking part. Churches in the States sent candy and small gifts for Christmas like pencils and coloring books. We played basketball, soccer, and other ball games, and did a lot of racing around."

■ ■ ■

During the revival some Armenian young people in the Old City pounded the church door with rocks.

■ ■ ■

Berge remembers the tremendous influence the Nazarene church and school had on his life. "I was brought up to read my Bible and pray every day as the result of my training," he says. "After graduating from the Armenian Evangelical Protestant School, I attended Bishop Gobat High School. However, I was not converted until my second year in high school during an old-fashioned, Holy Spirit-led revival at the church that lasted eight weeks. The church had spent much time in fasting and prayer before evangelist Timothy Chorbajian arrived from Beirut. He was Spirit-filled and knew the Bible.

"During the revival some Armenian young people in the Old City pounded the church door with rocks. But many of these, convicted of their behavior, joined the church services and found Christ. I was under conviction for several days before the Wednesday night service of the third week. I knew what I should do. When the evangelist asked us to bow our heads and lift our hands if we needed to be saved, I started praying while still seated and invited Jesus into my heart. Instantly, I knew my sins were forgiven and I was a child of God. Eight months later I was sanctified and felt the call into the ministry."

God not only answered Guelenia's prayer to help her family make the journey to Jerusalem so they could attend a holiness church but also used the Church of the Nazarene to reach both her husband and son for Christ.

■ ■ ■

**"I grew a mustache to look older.
And it worked!" Berge declares.**

■ ■ ■

A couple of years after graduating from high school at age 20, Berge returned to the Armenian Evangelical Protestant School as a teacher. He was concerned that some of the students who had started school at an age older than six might not pay attention to a teacher so close to their own age. Berge found the solution. "I grew a mustache to look older. And it worked!" he says.

The young teacher taught the whole spectrum of kindergarten to sixth grade. The curriculum included marching and simple exercises for the kin-

Doris and Berge Najarian, circa 1967

dergartners, while the elementary grades studied arithmetic, English, geography, science, history, Bible, penmanship, drawing, and physical exercise. His year as a teacher ended when he followed his sister, Louise, to the United States in 1947 for further training at Eastern Nazarene College (ENC). By this time Berge's parents had moved to Nablus, where Samuel worked as a pharmacist at the Anglican Church Missionary Hospital. Samuel and Guelenia also migrated to the States in 1947.

* * *

It might seem like the tale of the journey to Jerusalem has ended. Not so. While Berge was at ENC, he met Doris Roberts from Newfoundland. Af-

The Najarians, circa 1998

ter Berge graduated in 1950, he and Doris were married a year later. Berge completed his studies at Nazarene Theological Seminary in 1954, and then, after pastoring in Florida for six years, Berge and Doris were appointed as missionaries, arriving in Beirut, Lebanon, in 1960. Berge taught at the Bible school and pastored the Ashrafiyya Armenian Church.

In 1961 Berge once again would make a journey to Jerusalem, for he and Doris were transferred to the Holy Land District, which included all of Jordan, the West Bank, East Jerusalem, and the Old City. The Najarians served on the Holy Land District until 1976, when they were transferred to the Leeward/Virgin Islands District in the Caribbean. After 25 years of missionary service, they retired in 1985.

* * *

Until the 1948 Arab-Israeli War the work of the Church of the Nazarene was focused around the Armenian refugees in Jerusalem. Following this conflict, Jerusalem was divided. The Nazarene property housing the Armenian Evangelical Protestant School was, at that time, under Israeli control, and the authorities would not allow a church to be built under their jurisdiction. In 1973 the General Board finally decided to sell this property. The buildings were demolished by the new owners, and today a high-rise stands in place of the Armenian school.

The money Alvin Kauffman had raised for the Jerusalem church sanctuary was used to build a church in Nazareth in 1961. Later, the church in Jerusalem was revived and a large church facility was built on Nablus Road near the Garden Tomb. Outreach meetings are held in a small chapel in the Old City Armenian Quarter near the Jaffa Gate.

One thing is clear: God used the presence of Armenian Protestant refugees in Palestine to open the work of the Church of the Nazarene in Jerusalem. The British governor of Palestine, Sir Storrs, allowed the church to begin work in Jerusalem only because there was no Armenian Protestant church in the country. The opened door in Palestine would lead to the opening of the Church of the Nazarene in Jordan and Lebanon after the scattering of the Jerusalem congregation in 1948.

Only God could take such horrible historical events and use them to build His Church and to make a difference in the Middle East.

1. J. Fred Parker, *Mission to the World: A History of Missions in the Church of the Nazarene Through 1985* (Kansas City: Nazarene Publishing House, 1988), 383.

2. Parker, *Mission to the World*, 383-84.

2
Across the Jordan River

The brittle, yellowed newspaper clipping dated February 6, 1947, seemed too plain to be signaling a news flash. It had no byline, no accompanying photograph, no promise of new revelations in tomorrow's edition. Nothing gave a hint of the feat of courage it heralded. The small headline simply announced, "In Reverse; She's Going to Palestine." A two-inch story followed:

> While women and children are being evacuated daily from Palestine by the R.A.F. and civil planes, a woman flew out from Prestwick [Scotland] Airport today to settle in the Holy Land. She was Mrs. Grace Russell, who left with her husband, 38-year-old Rev. William Russell, a Wesleyan[1] missionary, for Cairo. "Where God calls, he will also protect," said the Rev. Russell as he stepped aboard the plane.

Not only was it the Russells' first journey by air,

---

1. Some people in the British Isles thought the Church of the Nazarene was Roman Catholic. Therefore, the words "Wesleyan" or "Wesleyan in doctrine" were often added to better identify Nazarenes.

but also they were the first British missionaries to travel by airplane to their assignment; previous missionaries had traveled by ship. William described their journey and arrival in the Holy Land in a letter to his home district.

■ ■ ■

**"Grace and I are surrounded with
barbed wire and plenty of soldiers."**

■ ■ ■

The Lord answered prayer in a wonderful way. Grace and I found air travel very comfortable and interesting. Our plane left Paris on Saturday with about 40 passengers. The lunch served in our hour's layover in Tunis was most welcome, as we had left without a proper breakfast. During our journey we were offered a free glass of whiskey—which we refused. We finally arrived in Cairo on Saturday evening. We reported to Air France on Sunday morning and discovered we had been booked to fly to Lydda, Palestine [present-day Lod, Israel], at noon. Although we hated traveling on Sunday, we felt it was best to go right through. Our flight took two hours. We had no trouble clearing immigration and were told to report back in three months. How amazed we were when we later found out that this would not be necessary, as we had been accepted as immigrants to Palestine, even though most Britishers had fled the country. Truly our

William and Grace Russell going to Jerusalem, 1947

God is a great God, for even the governments of the world are beneath His control.

The Nazarene compound is in a restricted area in New Jerusalem, so it was necessary for us to apply for permission to stay here. We [Grace and I] are surrounded with barbed wire and plenty of soldiers. I am writing this in a room facing King David's Hotel.

What led to this story of unsung heroism? Why did this unassuming couple choose to head straight

32

for a war zone? Because obedience to God's call was their main concern, not the issue of safety.

William Russell was born in Dublin, Ireland. He felt the call to the Muslim world while a student at Emmanuel College in Birkenhead, England, and later continued to prepare himself for ministry at Hurlet Nazarene College near Glasgow, Scotland (now Nazarene Theological College in Manchester, England). Before this journey to Jerusalem, William was pastor of the church in Dunfermline, Scotland. His London-born wife, Grace, was a nurse-midwife. She, too, had felt God directing her to be involved in missions. The Russells, appointed as Nazarene missionaries to Arab Palestinians in 1946, were assigned to work with Samuel Krikorian, the superintendent of the Nazarene work in Jerusalem.

■ ■ ■

William decided just to play it safe and wear his clerical collar from then on.

■ ■ ■

The day after the Russells arrived they registered in an Arabic language course. Those next months were traumatic. Fighting surrounded the area where they lived in the Old City of Jerusalem. Ten months later on November 29, 1947, following the United Nations recommendation to partition Palestine into Arab and Jewish states, the Arab-Israeli conflict exploded. Safety and job security became fleeting memories. En masse, Jerusalem Nazarenes joined the exodus of hundreds of thousands of Arabs and non-Jews to Transjordan (now Jordan), Syria, Lebanon, Egypt, and the United States.

With the scattering of the congregation and the imminent closure of the Jerusalem work, Samuel Krikorian and William Russell decided early in 1948 to explore the possibility of working with Armenian refugees across the Jordan River in Amman, Transjordan.

One morning the two men met for breakfast. As they left the restaurant a non-English-speaking policeman asked to check William's passport. He decided William was a Jew and took him to the Amman police station. A large crowd gathered, shouting, "Jew! Arrest him!" The officer in charge, fluent in English, was most upset about this accusation. He gave William a note of identification in case he had any further trouble. William decided just to play it safe and wear his clerical collar from then on.

While in Amman, Samuel heard about an Armenian family living in Zerka, a town of 5,000 people about 25 miles from Amman. (Zerka is on the edge of the Syrian desert in ancient Gilead country. The town is built beside the Brook Jabbok, where Jacob wrestled with the angel.) The two men decided to call on the Tashjian family: Samuel and Helen and their five sons—Jirair, Zaven, Kegham, Vahram, and Varouj. The missionaries explained they were with the Church of the Nazarene in west Jerusalem. They discussed their fears about possible adverse effects of the ending of the British Palestine Mandate and the proclamation of the state of Israel.

"Many members of the church as well as students in the school have already fled with their families to safer areas," the missionaries said. "And the possibility of the new Israeli state refusing to issue residence permits to non-Jews is real. The political situation is forcing the closure of the Jerusalem church and school, so we are considering starting a new school and church in Amman."

"Oh, yes," the Tashjians said immediately, "please establish this new Nazarene work in Zerka. There is a desperate need for an evangelical church and school in this place. Our three older sons are of school age. But because of our painful, personal memories of the Turkish treatment of Armenians, we've refused to send them to a public school, because Islamic teachings dominate and the Koran is the basic textbook."

■ ■ ■

Puzantohie and her sisters had escaped enslavement in a Turkish harem by rubbing dirt on their faces and disguising themselves as old women in their flight from Turkey.

■ ■ ■

The Tashjians' arguments were so persuasive that the decision was made for the Russells to transfer to Zerka and open a church and school. Samuel and Helen Tashjian were overjoyed, for now their boys could be educated in a Christian environment.

In April of 1948, one month before the new na-

The Russells with Ruth and baby Elizabeth in Zerka

tion of Israel was born, William and Grace Russell moved to Zerka, the dusty, desert outpost of the Arab Legion. The landlord of the mud-and-straw brick house they rented boasted about the good supply of water and electricity that would be available. It was an empty boast in the truest sense: water trickled from the faucet only occasionally, and electricity was available only a few hours a day. An oil lamp was used more often than not. Purchasing land and building adequate facilities—to include housing for staff, a church, and a school—would be necessary.

Once settled in their own home, William rented a building with mud-brick walls and concrete floors in the north central part of Zerka for the church and school. The first Sunday School classes were held in May 1948 with 31 children in attendance, most of them Arabs. That afternoon 18 adults gathered for the first Nazarene worship service. Sunday School attendance climbed rapidly, averaging 130 by the end of the year, and church attendance more than doubled. A Nazarene church with 12 members was organized less than two years later on March 12, 1950.

"At first we felt it would be impossible to open an elementary school," William says, "as neither of us had any teacher training. Help was to come, for by this time the Jerusalem Armenian school had closed for good and its teachers unemployed."

Puzantohie Yardumian, Hranoush Krikorian's sister, had been the head teacher at the Nazarene Armenia school in Jerusalem. Thirty years before, Puzantohie and her sisters had escaped enslavement in a Turkish harem by rubbing dirt on their faces and disguising themselves as old women in their flight from Turkey. Miss Yardumian received her teacher training in Beirut, and she was an excellent instructor, a true prayer intercessor, and woman of God. After the close of the Jerusalem school, she had moved to Zerka with her mother and dentist brother in a search for safety and stability. She was willing to organize the school and visit Armenian families in the area. Only with her knowledge, experience, and support was the Zerka Elementary School a viable project.

William tackled the task of registering the school. "I believe that God truly intervened during one important interview," he says. "The minister of education needed to give permission before the school could officially open. This was not the best time in the world for an American-based church to ask for government approval, since the Arabs in Transjordan were extremely angry with the Americans and the British. Arabs thought the Westerners were favoring the new Jewish state in the Arab-Israeli War. The minister of education could only be described as unfriendly when we met. His first question was abrupt. 'Are you American or English?'

"'Neither!' I quickly replied. 'I come from the city of Dublin in the Irish Republic.'

"The Minister laughed as he replied, 'de Valera [prime minister of the Republic of Ireland] hates the English too!'

"I thought of that old proverb, 'A closed mouth catches no flies,' and didn't respond. To my relief, the minister gave the Church of the Nazarene permission to open a school."

Classes began immediately with about 100 students in attendance—a mixed group of Muslims, Armenians, Catholics, Greek Orthodox, and Protestants. Grace Russell told of how the school opened doors into the community: "It offered great opportunity to teach children scriptural truth and Christian living. The school allowed us to reach out to the people of Zerka, for we can gain entrance into homes by visiting the families of children who miss class. The importance of hospitality in the Arab culture serves to make parents responsive and receptive to home visits built around their children." By the time the Russells returned from their first furlough in 1953, the work of the church and school in Zerka was firmly established.

The Russells believed they had escaped from the tension and trauma of war-zone living when they moved to Zerka in 1948. Not so! Despite the fact that the Baghdad Pact was opposed by other Arab League nations, Jordan signed it in 1955. The result? Riots broke out all over the country.

■ ■ ■

All air service to and from Jordan had been suspended, and the sale of petrol was forbidden to civilians.

■ ■ ■

Then in March 1956, young King Hussein dismissed the commander of the Arab Legion (Jordanian army) and ousted the British soldiers from the country. Later in 1956 the Egyptian president, Gamal Nasser, nationalized the Suez Canal. Great Britain and France banded together with Israel to oust Nasser and seize control of the Canal. The Suez-Sinai War began in October of that year.

Early in 1956 the Russells had been warned to be ready to leave Jordan on short notice. Because the situation seemed quiet, the fall school term at the

William Russell at home in England

Zerka Nazarene School began as usual. But the Russells were soon caught in the conflict between Britain and Jordan.

On the evening of October 31, William had an unusual experience. "I felt strangely compelled to fill the tank of our Plymouth Suburban with petrol [gasoline]," he says. "The next morning we learned that all air service to and from Jordan had been suspended, and the sale of petrol was forbidden to civilians. Shortly afterwards a telephone message came from our district superintendent, urging us to head for the Bible school in Beirut immediately. We hurriedly packed and set out for Lebanon, loaded to capacity. We expected trouble crossing the border, but to our surprise, we had no difficulties. In fact, all the officials were extremely kind to us. When we arrived in Beirut at 10 P.M., we were met by Donald Reed, school principal, and a crowd of happy students, who told us they had prayed most of the day for our safety. Once again we have proved that our God hears and answers prayer."

After just a few days in Beirut, the British ambassador to Lebanon called and strongly advised the Russells to return to Britain. They arrived home on November 14, 1956, having served in Jerusalem and Jordan for almost 10 years. Their dream of returning to the land and people they loved so much never materialized. Eventually, William took a pastorate and Grace continued working as a nurse-midwife. In July of 1996, soon after celebrating their golden (50th) wedding anniversary, Grace was called home to heaven. William is retired and lives in Brixham, Devon, England, in a flat near his daughter, Elizabeth.

Some might say 10 years isn't that long, at least not by society's calendar. But God used the Russells in those years of ministry in an unusual way. Students from the Zerka school still remember and talk about the remarkable influence and role model of William and Grace. Both the Zerka church and school continue to have a strong Christian presence in a town now populated by a half million people.

The church today is reaping the rewards of the Russells' decision to set aside their fears, venture into that 1947 Jerusalem war zone, and then to establish the Church of the Nazarene among Muslims in 1948. That headline 10 years ago really did herald feats of courage that would make a difference on both sides of the Jordan River and throughout the Middle East.

3
A Family Affair

Jirair, the oldest of the Tashjian boys, vividly remembers the momentous day in 1948 when Samuel Krikorian and William Russell visited his family in the west part of Zerka, Transjordan. Their simple house had mud-brick walls; a bamboo roof with mud plaster on top, supported by a beam at the center of the ceiling; a concrete floor; and an outhouse in the back yard with a hole in the floor.

All nine-year-old Jirair really wanted to do was go to school. But his parents refused to let him or his other two school-age brothers attend public schools. Both of his parents had fled Tarsus, Turkey, during the 1915 Armenian massacres. No way were they sending their boys to a public school steeped in Islam. A neighbor sometimes tutored the boys in the Armenian language for an hour or two a day. But Jirair didn't think of that as "going to school." He could hardly wait for the Russells to move to Zerka and open the promised Christian elementary school.

Jirair and two of his brothers, Zaven and Kegham, were the first students to enroll in the new Zerka Nazarene Evangelical School when it began classes in May 1948, right after the Russells arrived. Since the Tashjians spoke Armenian at home, the boys struggled those first few months, since the teachers and most of the students were Arabs and all the instruction was in Arabic. Eventually they did become the top students in their classes.

■ ■ ■

"We loved that rich, chocolate brew, but the porridge was another matter!"

■ ■ ■

Jirair has fond memories of his early student days. "The school yard was enclosed with a mud wall," he remembers. "Since lawns were unknown in Jordan, clouds of dust flew everywhere as running, screaming kids played during recess. During break time we students were served hot cocoa or porridge [oatmeal]. We loved that rich, chocolate brew, but the porridge was another matter!"

In addition to regular classes, Armenian students were required to take Armenian language and history from Puzantohie Yardumian, the sister of Mrs. Samuel Krikorian. "At the time," Jirair admits, "I resented this extra school load. But looking back, I consider myself fortunate that I had the opportunity to learn about my Armenian heritage from a person who knew so much of our story. She was determined not only to teach us to speak and write in Armenian but also to make us proud of our Armenian identity. In spite of her great commitment and enthusiasm as a teacher, she did have a few shortcomings that got on our nerves. Having never been married, sometimes she treated all Armenian children as if they were *her* kids. For example, she

43

Samuel and Helen Tashjian in front with their sons.
(L. to r.) **Vahram, Kegham, Jirair, Zaven, and Varouj.**

would get on our case if my four brothers and I played a little soccer on Sunday afternoons."

Jirair's brother Kegham recalls a time some years later when he and two younger brothers had greatly displeased Miss Yardumian, so she complained to Pastor Kamal Qusuus's wife. With a chuckle, Mrs. Qusuus told Kegham's father Miss Yardumian's complaint: "These Tashjian boys are acting worse than the Arabs." Miss Yardumian apparently had her prejudices, but interestingly enough, she was quite oblivious to the fact that Mrs. Qusuus herself was an Arab!

"When we come to know people as persons, they're no longer just Arabs," Jirair says. "In fact, some of the best friends that my parents and my brothers and I had were Arabs, from both Christian and Muslim families."

The establishment of the church went hand in hand with the development of the school. Regular Arabic services were started on Sunday mornings with Mr. Russell, as he was affectionately called, doing the preaching. George Kuttab had a significant role in conducting the Arab services as well as teaching at the school and assisting in its administration. On Sunday afternoons an Armenian service was held, with the Krikorians driving in from Amman to conduct the service.

■ ■ ■

Samuel Tashjian stood up, his hands visibly shaking while holding onto the pew, and prayed a prayer of confession and repentance.

■ ■ ■

In 1950 an American-Armenian evangelist by the name Helen Mooshian preached at the Armenian service. That sermon changed 11-year-old Jirair forever. "When she gave the invitation at the end of the sermon," Jirair says, "I don't know what made me do it, but I raised my hand along with others. I had attended school and church for two years by then and had heard enough teaching and preaching to know that a person needed to receive Jesus Christ as Savior. Miss Mooshian invited us to come to the altar to pray. I went forward, knelt at the altar, and started praying the Lord's Prayer. Rev. Krikorian explained to us a little more about the meaning of what we were doing. Then he led us in a simple prayer, asking Jesus to come into our hearts. On the way home I still remember the sense of utter exuberance. I felt as if I was walking on air. Life has not been the same ever since."

Jirair's accepting Jesus as his Savior disturbed his father greatly. He was restless and in much turmoil. He kept wondering how it was that his 11-year-old son felt the need to give his life to Christ, yet he, a 55-year-old man, had not done so. He determined he would take that step of faith and commit his life to Christ the next week. He could hardly wait. But when the following Sunday came, the service ended without an evangelistic appeal. He had to wait another week. The next Sunday, when the opportunity was given after the sermon, Samuel Tashjian stood up, his hands visibly shaking while holding onto the pew, and prayed a prayer of confession and repentance.

Kegham tells this story: "A week later, some friends came to visit us after church on Sunday evening. At the time I was 7 years old. My father asked me to offer a cigarette from a packet to the guests—a common courtesy still practiced in Jordan today. In the process I skipped my father. He then asked me for a cigarette. As I approached him I said, 'I thought after you repented you wouldn't smoke any more.' Late that night, my father went out into the moonlit yard, tore up all the cigarettes in his possession, and promised the Lord never to smoke again. After having smoked for over 30 years, often two packs a day, he never smoked again."

Jirair says that another milestone in his spiritual

journey was his decision to be baptized. "In countries that are not predominantly Christian," he says, "baptism is a much more serious step of faith and commitment than in the West. It was presented to me as a lifetime commitment to Christ and the Christian way; it was compared to a marriage covenant. The baptismal candidate was making a public declaration that, from this point on, there was to be no wavering, no second thoughts, no turning back. Was I willing to give myself to Christ in uncompromising, total, absolute surrender? As a young person in my early teens, I said yes, not fully realizing all the implications of such a decision."

The church rented a rickety bus for the ride down to the Jordan River, more than 1,000 feet below sea level. Samuel Krikorian performed the sacrament, assisted by William Russell. The whole family eventually accepted Christ and joined the Church of the Nazarene.

The town of Zerka, growing rapidly, swelled to a city of 70,000 by 1956, largely because of the enormous influx of Palestinian refugees. The Tashjians had moved near the railroad tracks on the other side of the main highway near a huge field, which provided the boys plenty of room to run around. One day the Tashjians watched hundreds of tents being set up on their open playground. It was to become a refugee camp for displaced Palestinians. As each family arrived, they were assigned a tent. Only public rest rooms and baths were available. Water for cooking had to be hauled to each tent from a central location. The conditions were deplorable. Some of the refugee children began to attend the Nazarene school and Sunday School. Those were exciting days of growth, expectation, and fellowship.

In a few years the church and school outgrew their rented property. Through Samuel Krikorian's tireless efforts, property was purchased just a few blocks away. Sometimes Jirair and his brothers would play in the empty field where the future facilities would be built. It was as if they were claiming the Promised Land!

Construction finally began on two stone-and-concrete buildings in 1954. Watching the masons chiseling away on the building blocks became a new pastime for the children. "My brothers and I helped to paint some of the window frames," Jirair remembers.

Finally the day came when the first two buildings were completed: a single-story school and a two-story edifice that housed the pastor on the top level and the caretaker on the ground floor. As it turned out, Samuel Tashjian took on the job of caretaker, his family delighted to move into modern facilities. The Russells were their upstairs neighbors until they were forced to return to England in 1956.

Samuel Tashjian continued to work at his regular job at the Arab Legion canteen, and in the evenings and on Saturdays he performed custodial duties at the school and church. He conscripted his five boys to help him clean the building, but he always took on himself the undesirable task of cleaning the toilets. Saturday afternoons and evenings were spent converting a couple of classrooms into a church sanctuary. Student desks had to be moved out and church pews moved in; then on Sunday evenings the process was reversed. For many years Samuel also served as the church treasurer.

Helen Tashjian kept busy being the mother of five active, growing boys. She was also heavily involved in the activities of the Zerka church and school during their first 10 years of existence. She played the pump organ in church and always sang while she played. During one service, as she "performed" with her usual enthusiasm and joy, a fly flew straight into her mouth. The violent fit of coughing that followed made her incapable of keeping up with the song; the whole church stopped singing and waited for her to clear her throat. She finally coughed up the unwelcome intruder and continued on with the song.

■ ■ ■

"Father came and found me and began to sob as he shared the doctor's diagnosis."

■ ■ ■

Helen was also involved with school music classes, teaching two-part harmony to the choir. The children performed in church as well as in the school's special events. Helen also served as the unofficial first-aid lady. She was always comforting children and bandaging their minor cuts and bruises. Kegham still remembers the neighborhood mothers telling their children to go to Mrs. Helen for a remedy for their pain. She especially loved the girls at the school as she did not have any daughters. She treated all the children as if they were her own.

The Nazarene school in Zerka offered classes only through the sixth grade. "Although my family was dirt poor," Jirair remembers, "my father felt that, after completing their elementary education, his sons should attend the best school available. All five of us boys would eventually graduate from the Anglican Bishops School, one of the best high schools in Amman."

In 1957 a dark cloud gathered over the Tashjian family. Helen began to be plagued with bouts of sickness. Numerous visits to the doctor did not alleviate her suffering. "My mother's health deteriorated," Jirair says. "Eventually, in January of 1958 when it was too late, she was diagnosed with cancer of the stomach. I was cleaning in the school when my father found out. He came and found me and began to sob as he shared the doctor's diagnosis. My mother was taken one more time to a Catholic hospital in Amman for some experimental drugs. A few days later my father brought her back home. She was delirious, unable to speak, suffering excruciating pain. We sat by her bedside, helpless. Finally, in the middle of the night, she found her final rest. I still remember the words I said as she breathed her last, 'Mother, give our greetings to Jesus.'"

The next day Jirair and his father went to a carpenter and asked him to make a casket. There were no funeral homes, no embalming facilities, no neat cemeteries in Zerka. "I will never forget that day," Jirair says. "Two hundred people packed the sanctuary

Zerka Nazarene school. Principal Jirair Tashjian
is standing on far right at top.

for Mother's service. I was amazed that a good number of my high school class had come all the way
from Amman. The long funeral procession walked
for 20 minutes to the cemetery north of the church.
Our mother was placed in an unmarked grave, since
we had no money to buy a tombstone, and I believe
her place of burial is forever lost. But the comforting
thought is that even if her grave is not known, she
could never be lost from the sight and love of our
Heavenly Father."

Jirair's involvement with the Zerka school was
not yet over. After high school graduation, the mission director appointed Jirair the principal of his al-
ma mater. "I can't imagine now how a 19-year-old
could be the principal of a school with 150 students

and six to seven teachers," he confesses. "In those days none of the teachers in the Zerka school had completed high school. Since I had a high school education, I suppose that was considered sufficient qualification to become a teacher and principal." He served in that capacity for one year before leaving for America to further his education.

■ ■ ■

Brother Bshara expressed his devotion to the Lord: "O let me kiss Your beard, Jesus!"

■ ■ ■

"An incident at the beginning of the school year made me realize how vulnerable I was as a teenager," Jirair remembers. "I had worked for days on a schedule of classes and teachers. The problem was that no one wanted to take the kindergarten class. Finally, after several futile attempts to assign a teacher to the young children, I realized no one was willing to teach them. I was angry, hurt, and frustrated. In desperation I ran home, threw myself facedown on my bed, and wept for a good long while. Eventually, I collected myself and decided who was going to handle the kindergartners. I completed a final schedule and informed the teachers of their assignments the next day. I explained that those who were unwilling to accept my decision could submit their resignation. No one quit, and the school year got under way.

"As I look back at the years I spent in the Zerka school, first as a student, then as teacher and principal, I can't help but be amazed that all of my teachers, with the exception of two, lacked a high school education."

What was it about this school that produced so many students who went on to high school, to higher education, and to effective careers at home and abroad? This school did not have many of the resources that are taken for granted and deemed essential for a good education these days. In spite of the scorching desert heat in the summers and bitter cold in winter, the classrooms were neither air-conditioned nor centrally heated. Most of the families had inadequate space for their children to find a quiet place to study. Some lived in tents. Yet, today there are graduates of the elementary school and members of the church youth group around the world, serving as physicians, nurses, veterinarians, professors, public school administrators, engineers, teachers, and ministers. The shortage of funds, appropriately trained teachers, conducive environments for learning, and appropriate teaching tools and materials were compensated for by the abundant unconditional love the students received from their teachers, parents, pastors, and community members. Though living in impoverished conditions, the children and teens all felt loved and that they were special.

"The first decade of the Zerka school and church," Jirair says, "was characterized by optimism, excitement, love, creativity, and a feeling that God was doing something marvelous in this place. A revival broke out one year in the late 1950s when an Egyptian evangelist preached to a sanctuary packed

Dr. Jirair Tashjian

with 200 or more people. Through the efforts of Jacob Amari a number of soldiers from the army were brought to the Lord. All-day prayer meetings were held during the revival. It was as if we had nothing else to do but sit around and pray. I still remember the prayer of Brother Bshara, who was a bit unconventional in the way he expressed his devotion to the Lord: 'O let me kiss Your beard, Jesus!'"

Today Dr. Jirair S. Tashjian is a professor of New Testament and Greek at Southern Nazarene University in Bethany, Oklahoma. "The influence of the Zerka Nazarene school and church had a deep impact on me," he says. "What I saw in the lives of William and Grace Russell—humility, gentleness, and a Christlike spirit—is a beautiful example of what holy living is all about. They were an inspiration to all who were influenced by their life and ministry. I will always be profoundly thankful that they followed God's leading and bravely ignored the political situation of Palestine in 1947; that they didn't give up when uprooted from Jerusalem by war; that they were willing to deal with the inconveniences of village living when they transferred to Zerka in 1948. They personified Jesus' love to us all."

Jirair, who made a difference in the Middle East, is continuing to make a difference on U.S. soil.

4
Beirut Blessing

Warnings. All Marlene heard about Protestant evangelicals during her growing-up years were warnings. She avoided friendships with members of those strange churches because they did not observe the traditions of her Maronite[1] Catholic family.

Marlene was raised with her sister and two brothers in Ain Zhalta, a town in the rugged, mountainous area of Lebanon. Even though her grandmother Bahia had attended the first evangelical school in that part of the country, Marlene remembers how her grandmother complained about the way her teachers had minimized the importance of Maronite Easter traditions.

"You know we Maronites celebrate Lent by fasting from eating meat," Marlene remembers her grandmother saying many times. Grandmother would go right on, ignoring the fact she had often reminded Marlene of the 40-day Lenten traditions. "Some of us also give up eggs, cheese, candy, or desserts. You know

---

1. Maronite Catholics trace their origins to St. Maron, a Syrian hermit of the late 4th century. A union with the Latin church was finalized in the 16th century. Since the establishment of a fully independent Lebanon in 1943, Maronites have constituted one of the two major religious groups in Lebanon.

the Easter traditions are very important to us. Those Evangelicals do not fast even one day for Lent."

"I always listened to Grandmother respectfully," Marlene says, "but I knew the Holy Week customs—very well."

On Maundy Thursday afternoon, Maronites visit seven churches. On Good Friday a man parades through village streets, dragging a cross with a crowd around him, much as Christ was surrounded on His march to Golgotha. Later in the day the man reenacts Christ's death by hanging on a cross, tied with ropes, for a few minutes. Some people sleep in the church on Friday night or walk barefooted to the Harissa Maronite Catholic Church, where a large statue of the Virgin Mary overlooks the city of Beirut. On Saturday the people attend midnight mass, anticipating the delicious meat dishes that will be served when the service is over. The replica of the tomb inside the sanctuary is covered with a black cloth for the Good Friday service. At the Saturday midnight mass a white cloth replaces the black one, and as worshipers exit the church, each person is handed a boiled egg with a scripture verse written on its shell. Then on Easter Monday the people enjoyed eating maamoul—a tasty cookie stuffed with either pistachio nuts, dates, or walnuts—during visits with their families and friends.

"Those Evangelicals don't think any of these activities are important at all!" her grandmother repeatedly criticized.

How can anyone find fault with such traditions, Marlene often wondered back then.

Marlene's parents, Salwa and Samir Mchantaf, were not believers[2] but they tried to do good and please God. They taught their children they could be saved and receive eternal life with good behavior. "At a very young age I understood that being good was extremely important," Marlene says, "and I did my best to be so."

High school years were spent at the Greater Beirut Evangelical School (GBES); still, she remained anti-Evangelical. After one of her friends became a believer, Marlene noticed her friend's new faith had changed her completely. She no longer went to parties or picnics with the guys. *She was stupid for letting her religious beliefs control what she does for fun!* Marlene remembers thinking.

■ ■ ■

"I knew my confession would be overheard by those waiting behind me, and I resented the lack of privacy."

■ ■ ■

Marlene became discontent with her traditional church. "Our family attended mass every Sunday, but the service bored me," she admits. "We sang the same monophonic [single-line melody] songs Sunday after

---

2. In the Arab Middle East, you are born into either a Christian or a Muslim family. When you accept Jesus Christ as your personal Savior you become a "believer."

Sunday." The priests and the congregation repeated the same prayers week after week. After years of repetition they became an exercise in memorization, not a method of communicating with God.

To take Communion, Marlene was required to fast before attending church. "Upon arriving at the church, I had to confess my sins to a priest," she says, "which meant listening to the confessions of others while I stood in line waiting my turn. I knew my confession would be overheard by those waiting behind me, and I resented the lack of privacy." So she began to take Communion only once a month to avoid this ordeal.

"As for the church offerings," Marlene acknowledges, "I really believed that the church was rich, so why did it need my contributions? I gave only small amounts, yet I had no idea how my offerings were used."

After Marlene graduated from GBES in 1983, she desired to study medicine in an east Beirut college near her home in Ashrafiyya. She entered a five-year program in nursing, which, up to that time, had been taught in English. But the year she applied, the school changed the teaching language to French. As do most Lebanese, she spoke some French, but most of her studies had been in Arabic and English. After attending classes only two days, she realized her French proficiency was too weak for this program. Frantically, she began to search for another college that taught in Arabic or English near her home, since the Lebanese civil war was raging and it would be unwise for her to travel too far from her area.

Soon after the Lebanese civil war began in 1975, the Lebanese University rented the Nazarene school building near Marlene's home for their Business Administration College. She enrolled. "I had no big desire to study business administration," she says, "but I started attending classes because I didn't want to just sit around and waste my time. One of the students was a believer, and I found him to be different from the others. He was helpful and trustworthy."

■ ■ ■

"What a predicament I was in—with no contract for either the bank or the school!"

■ ■ ■

In the middle of her first year of college, Marlene was asked to teach two classes of math in the

Abdo Khanashot and Marlene Mchantaf

Beirut Sin-el-Fil Nazarene School by the principal, Abdo Khanashot. She had attended high school with his daughter Laura. "Laura actually recommended me to her dad," Marlene says, "because she knew I had been a strong math student, that in fact I had tutored several students while I was in high school."

Although Marlene discovered she liked teaching, she didn't plan on making education her life's vocation. "At the end of the school year, Brother Abdo offered me a teaching contract for the 1984-85 school year," she says. "I refused, explaining that I had applied to work in a bank. I don't know what happened or how God's hand touched my situation, for even though I was well-qualified to work in the bank, I didn't get the job. What a predicament I was in—with no contract for either the bank or the school!"

In 1984 Lebanon had now been involved in civil war for nine years. The Sin-el-Fil school decided it was unwise to offer contracts to teachers for the coming year. But on the first day of school, Brother Abdo called Marlene and asked if she were free to teach math again in the morning.

■ ■ ■

**"I wanted to learn more about these people—
what made them tick!"**

■ ■ ■

Since Marlene's university courses were in the afternoon, she agreed to teach a combination of math and science classes for the elementary and intermediate grades. During this year, she realized the school administrators were not what she had expected. "Why, these people were nice to their staff and good to me," she says. "I felt loved and appreciated. Most important, they put no pressure on me to become an Evangelical, although they invited me to attend Nazarene services held at the school every Sunday."

At first Marlene told them she wasn't interested in attending their church. "But these Evangelicals seemed so different from the ones my grandmother talked about that I became curious," she admits. "I wanted to learn more about these people—what made them tick! I thought if I could understand that, I might find them to be exactly like those terrible Evangelicals I had heard so much about while growing up."

Marlene attended some Sunday services, just so she could better understand the people with whom she was working, to see if she should continue or quit her job. "At first, I was taken back by the Nazarene worship style," she says. "To begin with, there were no confessional booths at the entrance to the sanctuary. No icons, no photos, no statues of saints and the Virgin Mary were in sight. A simple cross behind the pulpit was the main item of decoration. And the sermons! In my Maronite experience I never heard an extemporaneous message geared to meet the spiritual needs of the congregation. I was used to memorized, written homilies repeated ceremony after ceremony. Bible readings were chosen by the Pope a year at a time. Rarely did the priest add anything or explain what these verses should mean to me personally. If anything, social or political issues were more important than spiritual instruction."

In Nazarene services, Marlene's heart responded most to the feeling of belonging—the bond between people who seemed to draw closer to each other as they grew closer to God. "I had never felt like I was a member of the Body of Christ in my Maronite worship experiences," she says.

The more Marlene attended church, the more she looked forward to the weekly biblical instruction. Her desire to learn more about the Bible forced this 19-year-old to study it for the first time. "Of course, as a student at evangelical schools in elementary and high school," she testifies, "I had memorized many portions of Scripture but never before had tried to understand what the verses meant."

■ ■ ■

Marlene realized that prevenient grace had been working in her life all along.

■ ■ ■

Gradually, Marlene began to grasp the true meaning of salvation, that it is not earned by good deeds or by taking Communion or by confessing her sins to the priest. Finally, she realized that salvation comes through Jesus Christ alone. "Suddenly I felt as if I were not a Christian," she acknowledges, "as if I were a person who knew nothing. The Holy Spirit revealed many things to me. As I began to attend all the meetings of the church, I started to have a new vision of the evangelical believer's life."

Students at the Sin-el-Fil Nazarene Evangelical School

In 1988 the Nazarene church had a revival. One night the evangelist explained how to be saved, how Jesus could change people's lives if they gave themselves completely to Him. "When I got back home," Marlene testifies, "I closed the door of my bedroom and wept. For the first time I decided I wanted to give my whole life to Jesus. I felt changed, that something new had happened in me. At last I experienced the true meaning of Easter and the importance of Christ's death and resurrection in a way my traditional celebration had never revealed."

As the eldest child in her home with important family responsibilities, Marlene faced many problems. Her father, who had lost his eyesight because of diabetes, was extremely depressed and refused to work at the family's shop every day as he used to. Twice he attempted suicide.

"I told my father about Jesus," Marlene says, "and how belief in Him could change his attitude toward life. After I shared this, my father was different. He started to enjoy life again. I told him how much we loved and supported him. Although he was shy about going with my mother to the shop, he found that people still respected and loved him. Our family life changed for the better."

"So many troubles came into my life during those dark days of war and my father's illness," Marlene says, "but I learned to commit everything to God. He gave me assurance that He could help me face any difficulty. I felt Him take my hand and lead me."

Marlene realized that prevenient grace had been working in her life all along—closing the door to medical school, missing out on the bank job, beginning to teach at the Nazarene school. All these events led her into a relationship with God. "I came to believe that life isn't about work or making money or holding high positions in big companies," she says. "God gave me a desire to teach children about Him, to tell them they don't need to wait until they are adults to develop a relationship with Him."

Marlene is now the assistant principal of Sin-el-

Fil Nazarene Evangelical School in Beirut. She joined the Church of the Nazarene in 1988. She is a board member and youth worker in her local church and serves as a member of the Lebanon District Advisory Board. In 1996 she began taking courses offered by the Eastern Mediterranean Nazarene Bible College in Lebanon, Jordan, and Cyprus to increase her understanding of theology and church history.

A dedicated administrator and diligent worker in God's kingdom, Marlene is totally involved in making a difference in her part of the world. Truly, Marlene Mchantaf is a Beirut blessing.

5
From Palestine to the Palace

Alex was only three years old in 1948, when the Abu Ghazaleh family fled the comfort of their ancestral home in Ramleh, Palestine. They landed in a tent in Jefnah near Ramallah for several months but eventually crossed the Jordan River and traveled up the mountains to Amman. The Abu Ghazalehs joined 700,000 other Palestinians fleeing to escape the dangers of the Arab-Israeli War. Few of these Arab refugees had any concept of the finality of this journey; they did not suspect that they would never again live in the land of their birth.

When it became obvious that going back home to Ramleh was impossible, Alex's father, Fayek, found work as a mechanic in the Arab Legion and moved his family to Zerka to be near the base. Because of the flood of refugees, only the poorest of housing was available. It was like a miracle when a British missionary organization offered them a brand-new, two-room clay home that had been built for Palestinian refugees right next to the Nazarene school. Fayek, raised Greek Orthodox, not Protestant, was quite suspicious of the motive behind this gift.

"Are you trying to buy me with this house?"

Fayek asked. "It won't work. I'm not going to become an Evangelical!"

"Not at all," was the reply. "Our records show that your grandfather gave land to our mission so that we could build a church, cemetery, and school in Ramleh. Now we are paying you back." Satisfied with that answer, Fayek accepted the house.

Father Abu Ghazaleh decided to send his five-year-old daughter, Suad, to the kindergarten class in the Nazarene school just next door, even though he personally thought evangelicals were heretics. Visits to students' homes were a part of the program of the Nazarene school. So Fayek was compelled to welcome the headmaster, William Russell, and other staff from the school who invited all of the Abu Ghazaleh children to attend Sunday School. By now, Alex had become best friends with Kegham and Vahram Tashjian, his neighbors that lived on the Nazarene compound because their father was the caretaker. When Alex asked if he could attend Sunday School just to be with his friends, his father reluctantly gave permission.

Though Alex attended public school, he would head straight for the Nazarene compound and his friends as soon as school was over. The Nazarene property was an unusual, out-of-the-ordinary place in Zerka. The mission staff had landscaped the land with trees and flowers and set aside a place for playing volleyball, basketball, and soccer. A favorite game was rounder, so named because a person hit a ball and ran "round" bases to home. After a hard-played game, the boys found it pleasant to sit in the garden, catch their breath, and cool off.

Eventually, Alex attended all the Arabic church services with the Tashjian boys. One hot summer evening all the boys lined up on the back pew to hear evangelist Eli Nuzha preach. Alex did not pay much attention to the message about the prodigal son. In fact, he remembers thinking the sermon a little strange. "But at the end of the message," he admits, "I found myself walking down to the altar to pray. I found Jesus as my Savior that night. My desire to be at the church grew. I was only home to eat my main meal and study. My mother became so angry with me. 'Why don't you just sleep there too?' she nagged."

Once in a while Miss Yardumian, the Tashjian boys' Armenian tutor, would catch Kegham and Alex playing in the school yard. She would corner them with these comments, "You're just wasting your time. Come over here and read from the English Bible with me."

■ ■ ■

Her creativity and vision were as foreign as *Star Trek* when compared to Jordan's traditional approach to education.

■ ■ ■

"We really wanted to run away from her," Alex remembers thinking. "It was like a kind of punishment, for we knew we would be 'caught' for hours. We wanted to play, not spend our time looking in commentaries to learn the meanings of English passages in the Bible. I later realized what a great lady she was, what a wonderful thing she had done in strengthening not only our English, but our knowledge of the Bible as well."

In 1957 Rev. Kamal Qusuus left his teaching position at the Nazarene Bible School in Beirut to become the pastor of the Zerka Arabic church. He also became Alex's spiritual father and encourager. At first he asked Alex to share for a few minutes in a Bible study. Later on Mrs. Muhab Qusuus trained Alex to be a Sunday School teacher. He eventually graduated to preaching during a worship service. Alex was a volunteer teacher during summer sessions at the Nazarene school. "We taught math and English and religion," he remembers. "No fees were charged for the classes. The purpose was to reach out to students who didn't normally attend the school."

Alex has high praise for Mrs. Qusuus. "She was not just a wonderful pastor's wife," he says. "She had studied with the British mission in Syria and was a remarkable teacher and very involved in the Nazarene school. Her creativity and vision were as foreign as *Star Trek* when compared to Jordan's traditional approach to education. The Nazarene school offered a physical education [P.E.] program, and students were taught game rules and skills to help them excel. In my public school we were collecting rocks during P.E. time. The Nazarene school and church produced big dramas of Bible stories and had a choir. Even the chief of police attended many performances. We really were the only act in town."

Alex had an ear for music and tried to accompany the worship services on the piano with a one-fingered rendition of the songs. A Nazarene from America named Mrs. Rice, whose husband worked for the Jordanian government in Amman, heard Alex's efforts and offered to give him piano lessons. "I had to go by bus to Amman for my last two years of high school," Alex says. "Mrs. Rice offered to pick me up after school once a week, give me a lesson, and then drive me back to the bus stop for the ride home. She said that she would provide all the music books and I could practice on the church piano. At first my father was totally against the idea, as he thought learning the piano would be a total waste of time. But since it cost him nothing, he finally agreed. She emphasized religious, not classical music, so I learned to sight-read hymns. I enjoy playing the piano for church services to this day."

Alex was the third son of a large family, and there was no money to spare for further study after high school. In those days it was unusual for young men of his society class to go abroad to study. Usually they went straight into companies or banks, and their salaries went to support their families. Alex was determined to continue his education, even though he had graduated from a public, not a private high school. He took the English language exam given by the American Embassy in Amman and received a score high enough to receive a grant of 75 Jordanian dinar (JD) to help with college expenses. He enrolled at the University of Cairo and spent JD15 for his airplane ticket. After arriving in Cairo, he survived on the remaining JD60 until his father could send him more funds.

"I was firmly established in my faith during those student days in Cairo," Alex says. "But when I first went to school, I didn't feel secure about my salvation, because someone in Zerka had told me if I couldn't speak in tongues then I wasn't really saved."

■ ■ ■

Alex never again doubted his salvation.

■ ■ ■

The pastor of the evangelical church Alex attended in Cairo was a true man of God. After Alex told the minister about his doubts, the pastor related the following story:

A man dreamed he was visiting the Israelites the day before the Exodus—the night before they were to flee from Egypt. He entered into one house and found the firstborn son trembling and terrified. "Why are you so scared?" the man asked.

"Haven't you heard about the death angel," the son replied, "who is going to come and kill all the firstborn sons?"

"Of course, but you put the blood on your door, didn't you?"

"Yes, but until I see the angel pass by, I'm not sure it will work!"

The visitor then entered another house and discovered the firstborn son to be in great spirits, full of singing and rejoicing that freedom was near.

72

"Don't you know that the angel of death is on his way?" the man asked.

"Yes, but it isn't a problem," the son answered. "The angel will pass over me, because the blood is on the house."

Then this wise pastor asked Alex a question. "Which son is the most secure?"

"The second son," Alex quickly answered.

"No, that's wrong," responded the wise pastor. "Both sons have the same security. Their security was not in how they felt but in the blood of Christ. It is like you. All your feelings have nothing to do with your redemption. Your redemption is through Jesus' blood shed on the Cross."

Alex never again doubted his salvation.

In January of 1970 Alex returned to Jordan a fully qualified veterinary surgeon with one aim and purpose: to own his own clinic and operating theater. But the political climate in Jordan forced him to delay his dream. Palestinian militants had tried numerous times to kill King Hussein, making Alex's Palestinian heritage a real disadvantage. Besides, he was a member of the Christian minority in a world controlled by Muslims. Black days followed with Alex unable to find work as a veterinarian. He finally began a job as a distributor for a pharmaceutical company, going from doctor's office to doctor's office, offering samples of new medicines and delivering orders. This he did for two years. Then the miracle happened.

In 1972 Alex was presenting some samples to a British pediatrician married to an important Jorda-

Dr. Alex Abu Ghazaleh

nian man. In the middle of his spiel the doctor inter-
rupted. "You have medical training, don't you?"

"Yes," he replied, and then described his training
as a veterinary surgeon.

"Can you operate on animals?" she asked.

"Of course. That's what I'm trained to do. I
don't have any instruments, but I could buy some."

"I have a friend who has three cats that need to
be spayed," she explained. "She can't find anyone to
do it here in Jordan, so she's planning to send them

74

to Europe for the operation. If you'll meet me here tomorrow morning, I will take you to her house and you can perform the operations."

"OK," he agreed.

Back home Alex dumped his medical samples out of his bag and rushed downtown to buy some forceps and other supplies. The next morning the doctor picked up Alex in her car, and they headed for her friend's home. Much to Alex's surprise, she turned into the wide gates leading up to the royal residences. She pulled up to an impressive building, stopped, and told Alex to get his bag. Who should answer the door but Princess Sarvarth and Prince Hassan, King Hussein's brother! What an experience that was, to have a princess hovering over him as he performed the three operations on the kitchen table. Alex prayed constantly during all the procedures. "Lord, don't let these cats die, or my reputation will be ruined at the very beginning of my career!"

"God is good, for all three cats survived my scalpel," Alex says. "I never dreamed that these successful surgeries would play any part in my future. Prince Hassan was impressed with my skills. He did not know it was my very first operations on my own. He even asked me to stay for lunch. Then 10 days later, I was introduced to His Majesty, King Hussein. He told me he was proud of me, and that he was happy to find a trained vet living in Jordan. He asked me if I would be willing to look after his animals. Of course, I said yes."

Soon after, an event occurred that spread the word about Alex's work and capabilities. "I received a call from the royal palace," he remembers, "asking me to go to the house of Mr. Balfour, the British ambassador. His trained German shepherd had been bitten by a poisonous snake and was dying. The palace actually sent a car to take me to the ambassador's residence. First, we went to downtown Amman, where I searched for the antivenin serum. I finally found some in an emergency medical center that treated people, not animals. I could tell the dog was near death when I gave him the shot. There I was again, praying for God to save another animal. And the next morning the dog was up walking around!

"His Majesty heard about my success and called me again and thanked me for my good work. But what is amazing is what the British Ambassador did. He called every ambassador in Amman and told them they needed to have me look after their pets. In this word-of-mouth testimony my practice grew practically overnight. I was soon able to resign my distributor's job and work fulltime in veterinary medicine."

■ ■ ■

King Hussein gifted Alex with some land near the Jordan University.

■ ■ ■

Alex went to Prince Hassan's palace in 1973 to treat an epidemic disease that had infected the gazelles. King Hussein was visiting his brother that evening. Alex was called inside to meet with His Majesty. "You've been working for us [the royal family] now for over a year, but you have not presented us with any bills," the king said. "I would like to give you something for your efforts. Princess Sarvarth suggested I give you a piece of land on which you could build a veterinary clinic, kennels, and a home. This will be good not just for the royal family, but for the country of Jordan." King Hussein soon gifted Alex with some land near the Jordan University.

Alex experienced difficulty in getting all the utilities needed to run a clinic. "Mine was the first house in the area," he says. "I paved the street for 500 meters (1,640 feet) from the main road to my house. I bought trucks of water and stored it in a cistern. Getting a phone line to the house and clinic was a huge problem. No telephone cables existed in those days. Though copper lines hung from wooden poles, each village was allowed only two lines. To contact me, people had to call the village of Swayla, which is just up the road a ways, and connect with an operator who would then connect them to me. But for most of my clients that wouldn't work; the operator only spoke Arabic. But the greatest percentage of my business came from non-Arabic-speaking foreigners.

"The telephone company refused to give me a private line, rigidly enforcing its policy of only two lines to a village." The royal palace intervened for me, and I finally got a private line at a cost of 1,500 Jordanian dinars—and my land was worth only JD2,500! To build my home and business, His Majesty King Hussein sent me a check for JD5,000, and I borrowed JD10,000 for the rest."

Alex still cares for the pets of the royal family. Recently, Princess Muna, the mother of King Abdullah, watched him operate on her tiny pug dog. Alex has received letters of appreciation from King Hussein and Queen Nour in the past, thanking him for his time and efforts with their animals through the years.

Alex remains active in the Church of the Nazarene in Jebal Amman. He became involved in the preaching ministry of the church after Pastor David Nuzha died on New Year's Day 1991. Alex is a favorite speaker in many of the Evangelical churches in Jordan.

"My life was so indelibly touched by the lives of those Nazarenes who came to Zerka—the Russells, the Krikorians, the Qusuuses, Miss Yardumian, and Mrs. Rice," Alex testifies. "And my friendship with the Tashjians played a big part in my exposure to my spiritual need and finding Jesus as Lord. What a difference all these made in my life and the others they touched through the work of the Church of the Nazarene in Jordan."

6
Worth It All

Alex Abu Ghazaleh thought it would be a usual procedure when Munir and his wife, Amera, entered his small animal clinic to have their pet terrier vaccinated. They had come upon the animal clinic during a walk in the neighborhood. The veterinarian introduced himself as Dr. Alex, and as he prepared the injection, the trio made polite conversation.

Alex learned this couple had fled their home and country in 1997. For two long years they had been anxiously waiting for visas so they could join their son in Canada. A dermatologist, Munir previously had a large private practice and taught at a university.

From the way the couple talked, at first Alex thought they were Christians. Then he discovered they were Mandaeans, followers of John the Baptist. Alex knew that Mandaeans, who call themselves Baptists, accepted Jesus and John the Baptist as prophets equal in stature, and that they believed in being baptized multiple times since they view baptism as a magical process giving immortality, purification, and physical health. The Mandaean Baptist religion has about 50,000 followers today, most of whom live in the Middle East.

Some of the Mandaean teachings parallel those of Christianity: the belief system is monotheistic, Sunday is a holy day, and marriage and children are held in great esteem. Other teachings differ. Strict control of diet is important; forbidden foods include mushrooms, fish without scales, beef, pork, rabbit, and camel.

Mandaean beliefs are full of myths, especially about John the Baptist, who, according to them, was not beheaded. Rather, they believe John lived to be an old man and was taken up to heaven alive, like Elijah, at the Jordan River. According to Mandaeans, John's ministry on earth definitely was not preparing the people for Jesus, the Messiah.

■ ■ ■

Munir and Amera had been wealthy once— owners of a beautiful home with a thriving clinic in the best business district of a large city.

■ ■ ■

Alex informed Munir and Amera that he was a believer in Jesus Christ and the Bible states John the Baptist came to prepare the way for Jesus. He explained that John the Baptist is quoted as saying he was not even worthy of washing Jesus' feet.

When Alex offered them a Bible, they actually accepted it and promised to read it, while commenting, "We refuse to accept that John admitted to be lower then Jesus. And we have our own holy book, the *Ginza*."

"What are you doing this coming Sunday?" Dr. Alex asked.

"Nothing," Munir responded. He went on to say, "Actually our lives are extremely monotonous right now, just sitting around and waiting for our visa applications to be approved. I'm not even allowed to practice medicine in Jordan."

"I speak on Sunday evenings at the Nazarene church in Jebal Amman," Alex said. "Would you like to come to church with me? You live close by, and I could pick you up." Out of boredom, the couple agreed.

The next three Sundays, Alex and his new friends visited as they traveled to and from church. During these rides, Alex learned a lot about them.

Munir and Amera had been wealthy once—owners of a beautiful home with a thriving clinic in the best business district of a large city. When they fled their country, they received only a fraction of the true value of their assets. And they had been fortunate to get that! Living in a furnished apartment in Amman had depleted their funds. Truly, life looked bleak, and depression, marked clearly on their faces, had settled on them.

"In those days I was greatly inspired and influenced by Philip Yancey's book, *The Jesus I Never Knew*," Alex says. "Yancey explores Jesus' personality and describes His character, His deity, His uniqueness in a clear way. I was using this book as a basis for my Sunday evening Bible studies. After the first service I asked Munir and Amera if they enjoyed themselves. Their response was neutral: 'It was fine, Dr. Alex.' I did not push them for any more feedback than that."

After Munir and Amera attended three Sunday evening services, the first Sunday of the new month arrived. It's the custom to celebrate Communion at the Jebal Amman Nazarene Church on the first Sunday of the month.

"You have to be careful tonight, because you will be serving Communion," Alex's wife, Huda, said. "You must instruct Munir and Amera not to share in this sacrament." On the way to church Dr. Alex explained that he would be serving Communion after the Bible lesson.

"What's Communion?" they asked. They had never even heard of it.

■ ■ ■

"My wife stared at me, her expression full of disbelief, her searing eyes charged with the message for me to do something."

■ ■ ■

Alex tried to describe in a simple way the meaning and purpose of the breaking of bread and drinking of wine, that this sacrament had been ordained by Jesus the night before He was crucified. "According to the apostle Paul," Alex continued, "no one should partake of Communion until he has confessed his faith and confidence in Jesus, until he has believed in Jesus' death and resurrection." Alex asked them not to participate, and then finished the discussion by stating, "Maybe one day you will become believers, and then you will be welcome to join in."

After presenting the Bible study, Alex asked those interested in taking Communion to come to the altar and front benches. "To my astonishment, Munir and Amera came forward!" Alex says. "My wife stared at me, her expression full of disbelief, her searing eyes charged with the message for me to do something. I couldn't stop them. I couldn't embarrass them in front of all the others. I felt like my only option was to serve them the elements, just as I did the others."

While headed for home afterwards, Alex had to contain himself to keep from lashing out at them, from asking them what in the world they thought they were doing. He was trying to think of the right words to say, but found it impossible to even open the subject of their participation in the Lord's Supper. Arriving at his friends' house, Alex pulled over for them to get out. Amera opened the door, but just sat there, not moving.

Suddenly she spoke. "Dr. Alex, today I felt I was born again. I'm a new person now. I believe in the blood of Jesus Christ and that He has washed my sins away."

Then Munir added, "I must tell you, I feel I was raised to another level in my faith tonight."

The Abu Ghazalehs sat, stunned, as the new believers left the car and entered their home.

Call it coincidence. Call it fate. Call it God's grace. But that week Munir and Amera received the news their visas to Canada had been issued and they had to leave Jordan in a week. They were so new in the Lord, Alex hated for them to leave. But they had no choice.

The Sunday before their departure, Munir asked Alex if he could share for a couple of minutes in the church that evening. He wanted to thank everyone for their kindness and support. Standing tall in front of the pulpit, he testified, "I declare, in front of God and in front of you all, that I believe in Jesus Christ as Lord. He is my Savior. We lived in a state of agony and depression for two years. Now we realize why the Lord delayed our visas. It was so we could meet Him and know Him. We believe the visas were issued in response to our new faith in Jesus. We lost everything in our country, but now I feel like we have won everything.

"This past week my son called me from Canada to tell me what a favorable time it is for me to be coming, that a big Mandaean Baptist conference is scheduled soon after we arrive, and that a high-ranking priest will be there to perform the important ritual baptisms. 'Son,' I told him, 'tell them I will not be baptized during these rituals, for I have been baptized with the Holy Spirit.'"

■ ■ ■

**But the Holy Spirit was leading them
forward by giant leaps!**

■ ■ ■

Amera then spoke from her place in the pew. "I spent two years mourning the loss of my house, my nice cars, my husband's business and career." For a moment she was silent. Then, her face awash with tears, she testified, "But if losing everything was the price we had to pay to know Jesus Christ, it was worth it."

After the service Alex asked Munir, "Where did

you get the idea that you have been baptized by the Holy Spirit?"

The answer was quick and sure. "This is what I felt when I read about John the Baptist, who said, 'I baptize you with water for repentance. But after me will come one who . . . will baptize you with the Holy Spirit and with fire' (Matt. 3:11). This is my experience when I met Jesus Christ. John the Baptist baptized me with water, but Jesus baptized me with the Holy Spirit. I don't need multiple water baptisms any more!"

Alex says, "Now I've been living for the Lord for 45 years, but I learned a powerful lesson through the testimonies of Munir and Amera. I was trying to lead them through their Christian walk with Jesus one small step at a time. But the Holy Spirit was leading them forward by giant leaps! Their testimony exposed the ability of the Holy Spirit to teach and direct and guide these new believers with a timetable completely different from mine."

Munir read his Bible voraciously. Every time he and Alex met, he questioned his friend about the meaning of Scripture verses. "Even when I took him to the airport, all the way to the check-in counter Munir was discussing spiritual things," Alex says. "I encouraged them to start attending church as soon as they arrived in Canada, which they did. Munir E-mails me regularly. They both remain strong in their faith and are growing in the Lord. Their most precious possession continues to be their faith in Jesus."

Dr. Alex Abu Ghazaleh, veterinarian extraordinaire, is a Nazarene who is making a difference in his world.

Pronunciation Guide

The following information is provided to assist in pronouncing some unfamiliar words in this book. The suggested pronunciations, though not always precise, are close approximations of the way the terms are pronounced in English.

Abdullah	ahb-DUHL-luh
Abu Ghazaleh, Alex	ah-BOO gah-ZAL-ee
Fayek	FAY-yak
Huda	HOO-duh
Suad	soo-AHD
Aintab	ien-TAB
Ain Zhalta	ien ZHAHL-tuh
Amari	ah-MAH-ree
Amera	ah-MEE-ruh
Amiralian, Mergerditch	ah-mee-RAH-lee-an MER-ger-dihch
Amman	ahm-MAN
Ashrafiyya	ahsh-rah-FEE-yuh
Bahia	BAH-hee-ah
Bludan	bloo-DAN
Brixham	BRIHKS-ham
Bshara	buh-SHAH-rah
Chamichian, Yevigne	chuh-MEE-chee-uhn yah-VEEN
Chorbajian	chohr-BAH-jee-uhn
DePasquale	dee-pahs-KWAH-lee
de Valera	deh vuh-LEER-uh
Dunfermline	duhn-FERM-luhn

Ginza	GIHN-zah
Gobat	GOH-bat
Harissa	hah-REES-sah
Hassan	HAS-suhn
Hussein	hoo-SAYN
Jaffa	JAHF-fuh or YAHF-fuh
Jebal Amman	JEH-buhl ahm-MAN
Jefnah	JEF-nah
Kauffman	KAHF-muhn
Khanashot, Abdo	KAHN-uh-shaht AHB-doo
Khartoum	kahr-TOOM
Krikorian	kree-KORH-ree-uhn
Kuttab	kuht-TAB
Lod	LOHD
Lydda	LIHD-uh
maamoul	ma-MOOL
Mamluks	mam-LOOKS
Mandaean	man-DAY-uhn
Marash	muh-RAHSH
Maronite	MEHR-uh-niet
Mchantaf, Marlene	muh-SHAN-tahf mahr-LAYN
Salwa	SAL-wuy
Samir	sah-MEER
Mooshian	MOO-shee-uhn
Muna	MOO-nah
Munir	moo-NEER
Nablus	NAB-luhs
Najarian, Berge	nah-JEHR-ee-uhn BERJ
Guelenia	goo-LEE-nee-uh
Higazoon	hee-gah-ZOON
Ohan	OH-han
Nasser, Gamal	NAH-ser gah-MAHL
Nour	NOOR
Nuzha	NUHZ-hah

Qusuus, Kamal	kuh-SOOS kah-MAL
Muhab	MOO-hab
Ramallah	rah-MAHL-lah
Ramleh	RAHM-leh
Sarian, Nerses	SAH-ree-uhn NER-sehs
Sarvarth	SAHR-varth
Sin-el-Fil	sihn-al-FIHL
Swayla	SWAY-lah
Tashjian, Jirair	TAHSH-jee-uhn juh-RAHR
Kegham	keh-GAHM
Vahram	VAH-rahm
Varouj	vah-ROUZH
Zaven	ZAH-vahn
Thahabiyah	thah-hah-BEE-yah
Yardumian, Hranoush	yahr-DOO-mee-uhn hrah-NOUSH
Puzantohie	poo-zan-TOO-hee
Zerka	ZER-kuh